A Christmas Diary

of ....

JUST IMAGINE ...

Snow-laden trees, wreaths at the windows, cookies

baking in the oven, the Christmas tree ablaze with lights ...

each a family tradition ... each a future memory of this

magical holiday season ...

A CHRISTMAS Diary

With text by
Judith Price

Photography by
Matt Schmitt and Sue Hartley

Design by
Morgan Williams & Associates, Inc.

Published by

Department 56
INC.

ISBN 0-9622603-5-5

Printed in the United States

HOLIDAY TRADITIONS

All our lives we follow traditions—do things the way our parents and grandparents did them. At the same time changing circumstances and lifestyles help us refine and begin new traditions for our children and grandchildren in a constantly changing circle. Christmas is a time when tradition takes on a most wonderful meaning for us all.

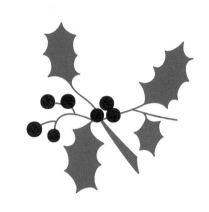

A HOLIDAY GREETING

Dear Friends,

When I was asked to share my Christmas memories I immediately thought of my own Christmas Diary — a journal I've kept over the years detailing the little moments and the big changes that have transpired in our celebrations.

my cousin and I — Christmas, 1946 . . .

must remember — plan an English tea — December, 1995 . . .

I have spent many happy hours, first capturing these precious times, then remembering them again as I reread each page. As our children have grown and started their families they have taken this tradition of a holiday journal with them. I hope you enjoy your Christmas Diary as much as I have enjoyed mine. . . .

As I paged through my journal, the first entry dealt with one of our first challenges as newlyweds — deciding whether our tree should be topped with an angel or a star.

Over the years we have celebrated Christmas in our hometown with our families only a precious 2 or 3 times. We have been anywhere from 500 to 5,000 miles from our roots and traditions. For several years there seemed to be so many babies, toddlers, and various pets in our house that we had to put the tree up Christmas Eve day and decorate it after the children were snug in their beds. Between decorating and putting together the tricycles and doll buggies, we would fall into bed just before the eldest child would tiptoe in to tell us breathlessly that Santa had indeed arrived.

Our wonderful tree — Christmas, 1969...

Our youngest son visits Santa —
December, 1980...

The years quickly passed and our bedtime became more and more reasonable — but tradition is tradition, so today we still put up our tree on Christmas Eve day. But now the baby is twenty; we are down to one little dog; and so we can decorate the tree during the day. We have neighbors in for mulled cider and fondue in the evening.

Traditions run so deeply — it's interesting to think about where they began. Our family's heritage is Welsh, English, Irish, German; I would assume most of our Christmas traditions come from Western Europe with a healthy helping of American custom. Because of an old Welsh legend, our children always put a lighted candle in the window to welcome the Christ Child. A plate of cookies and a glass of milk left by the hearth for Santa is purely American; and our son's concern for all animals led to the family practice of leaving raisins for the reindeer. My husband puts the lights on the tree, then everybody helps decorate it. The children invited friends over to help string popcorn and cranberries, but recently we switched to less time-consuming and more permanent beaded

a family tradition for many years...

garlands. We all love unwrapping the tissue from the ornaments; each one is a story. The colorful ornament a daughter made from yarn and Popside® sticks when she was a Brownie... the glistening snowflake my grandmother gave us our first Christmas... the little house from a neighbor with our name on the door... tiny painted angels a friend brought from Mexico... the origami cranes our daughter's Japanese college roommate made... the Snoopy a son baked when shrink-art was the thing... plus the few antique glass balls, still unbroken, from my husband's family and the fragile silvered horn my great-great-grandfather brought from Germany. The past few years we have nestled our Village in the snowy folds of a wedding gift tablecloth under our wonderful tree. These are our family's traditions and treasures, old and new, all part of the memories recorded in my Diary.

In the weeks before Christmas when we make cookies and other good treats, we use the recipes I have copied into my journal. Christmas Eve morning the children fill baskets with these gifts and deliver them to our neighbors. I have snapped their pictures and kept the photographs tucked into the pages of the Diary capturing their happiness as they come back with the baskets refilled with homemade presents given in return. This is a custom we brought with us to our present neighborhood and even though the children are grown, they still love doing it.

1994 — A very special Christmas with everyone home

Christmas morning we empty our stockings, and after breakfast we begin to open our presents, one person at a time, starting with the youngest. This way everyone gets to watch and enjoy. We call and talk to our family and friends and eat our Christmas feast in the evening. We toast the world, our family, our friends. Although the menu is always basically the same, as our family has expanded we have included new favorites from new members. The guest list varies with circumstances — the more, the merrier — there is always room to welcome another. Dessert must include my mother's fruitcake. After dinner we sing carols and reminisce.

Our end-of-the-evening is a fairly new tradition — begun one year when we had foreign guests. Conversation was difficult for the visitors, so we decided to play charades. The children loved it and we've continued every year — sometimes just the family, more often friends, neighbors, and anyone we know who needs a Christmas home.

Our family is still growing and changing… recently with the arrival of our first grandchild we have been blessed with the best of all Christmas traditions — a baby.

Through the years my constant companion at our Christmas celebrations has been my camera. Not only for the usual pictures of everyone holding their favorite present or dressed in their holiday best — I take pictures of everything! All the decorations … a close-up of the centerpiece, the arrangement of our Village, one year on the coffee table, the next on the mantel. The tree bedecked and splendid, the presents heaped underneath. The stockings hung and stuffed. The table set and perfect, the roast, the dessert, and the guests. These photographs have become the illustrations for my Christmas Diary, together with a journal where I have kept track of not just special memories of our holiday celebrations, but recipes and decorating and gift ideas gathered throughout each year for the next time.

Altogether I have an invaluable record, and now, this book will provide a record for our next five years… five years of Christmas memories. And, it is nice to think that you, too, will have your record of cherished memories for the years to come.

Judith Price
Ms. Lit Town

CHRISTMAS MEMORIES OF 19

Our memories keep our traditions alive. *A Christmas Diary* is a wonderful way to capture the spirit and traditions of this and future Christmases and save the memories for you and future generations. Christmas is a time for family and friends to gather together to share their blessings... to renew old friendships ... to welcome and nourish new ones. It is the time to honor the past and cherish the present... the time of good thoughts, generous wishes, and happiest expectations.

HOLIDAY HOME DECORATING

Start planning weeks in advance how you want to decorate your home ... how you want to trim the tree ... what you want to make ... what you'll need to buy ... should you have an open house or a caroling party ... go to church on Christmas Eve or Christmas morning ... who will meet the plane bringing out of town guests ... who will give the Christmas blessing? Start deciding what kind of card to send and who to send it to ... the perfect present for each of those on your list ... right down to what special and unexpected gift will be stuffed into the toe of a favorite relative's stocking.

In no time at all your house is filled with good Christmas smells—cookies baking ... bread rising ... fruits and spices ... fresh greens ... scented candles ... Presents are beautifully wrapped with that special touch and hidden away. The flowers are arranged; the silver is polished. The candles stand waiting to be lit amidst garlands of holly and ivy on the sideboard. Bowls of nuts and bright red apples are set about the house. Ropes of deep green pine swag the banister and strings of garnet-colored cranberries are ready to be looped around the tree.

THE NIGHT BEFORE
CHRISTMAS

Then it's Christmas Eve. Your house guests have arrived from near and far ... the children are wide-eyed and on their very best behavior. The tree is more beautiful than ever before as it stands tall and splendid, ablaze with lights that are reflected a thousand times in the treasured ornaments hanging from each branch. The gifts are brought from their secret places and carefully set about the beautiful miniature Village nestled in the frosty cotton landscape under this perfect tree. The logs stand waiting to be lit and the stockings hung by the chimney will be magically filled when morning arrives. Time for bed ... time to dream of ho ho hos and jingling sleigh bells.

CHRISTMAS
DAY

Christmas day has come at last...

the shining day.

Outside, Christmas bells are
ringing joyfully from the tall
white steeple of a church.
No matter what the weather...
it's always beautiful. Up and
down the street brightly colored
lights already shine—by dusk
they will guide and welcome
all who come to call.

Inside, the young children, dancing with anticipation,
are handing out the carefully tagged presents. The table
is waiting... best china on a lace tablecloth... the candles
and centerpiece... bright Christmas red napkins tied with
sprigs of holly... even the place cards are lettered and in
place. Everyone is dressed in their best... the little girls
in pretty velvet dresses... the gentlemen in their new
Christmas ties. What more beautiful time? Our memories
keep traditions alive. One of the special joys of the season
is the gathering of family and friends... children,
grandchildren, parents, and grandparents. It gives us the
perfect opportunity to tell stories and remember times past.

Holiday HOME DECORATING

Holiday decorations make a home a festive and welcoming place. For a special and personal touch, stack a group of beautifully wrapped packages on a child's old sled or wagon. Wallpaper printed with old-fashioned designs can be used as wrapping paper and will add to the antique look of your display. A snapshot attached in your Diary can be enjoyed by generations to come. Keep a record, too, of what you bought and where you bought it.

THE *Night* BEFORE
CHRISTMAS

When all is ready and waiting for the glorious day, the night before Christmas is the right time to photograph special things that you have decorated—the tree— the mantel—your Village—each room—even outside— the Christmas wreath on the door—the lights on the trees and shrubs. This helps plan for next year and also becomes a treasured memory for the future.

Our
CHRISTMAS
CARD

CHRISTMAS Day

A time to gather together. A little planning and a list of tasks to be assigned will make all your guests feel at home and everyone will have time to enjoy the day. Keep the menu low maintenance—a roast of beef or ham can be put in the oven and left until it's ready. Choose side dishes that can be prepared ahead or fixed quickly. Set the table early in the day, even the night before. When the last leftover has been refrigerated—the last guest waved goodbye— take five minutes and critique the dinner in your Diary. It will help make next year's dinner even easier.

The CHRISTMAS TABLE

One of the traditional joys of the holiday season is the gathering together of dear friends and family around the table for Christmas dinner. It is a feast for all the senses. The delicious aromas envelope the house and all within ... the sight of the gleaming silver, best china, and sparkling crystal reflecting in the candle glow ... the taste, soon to come, of tried-and-true favorite dishes as well as some new treat added for the first time ... Best of all, the anticipated delight of friendship and good conversation ... and dessert.

The
CHRISTMAS
MENU

Guests

Everyone enjoys Christmas dinner. The meal of the year ... it always lives up to expectations. The menu is decided weeks or even years ahead. Planning your menu down to the last detail gives you opportunities to try new ways of cooking and presenting old favorites as well as introducing new tempting ideas. Each year write your Christmas menu in your Diary. It will be a mouthwatering reminder of Christmases past.

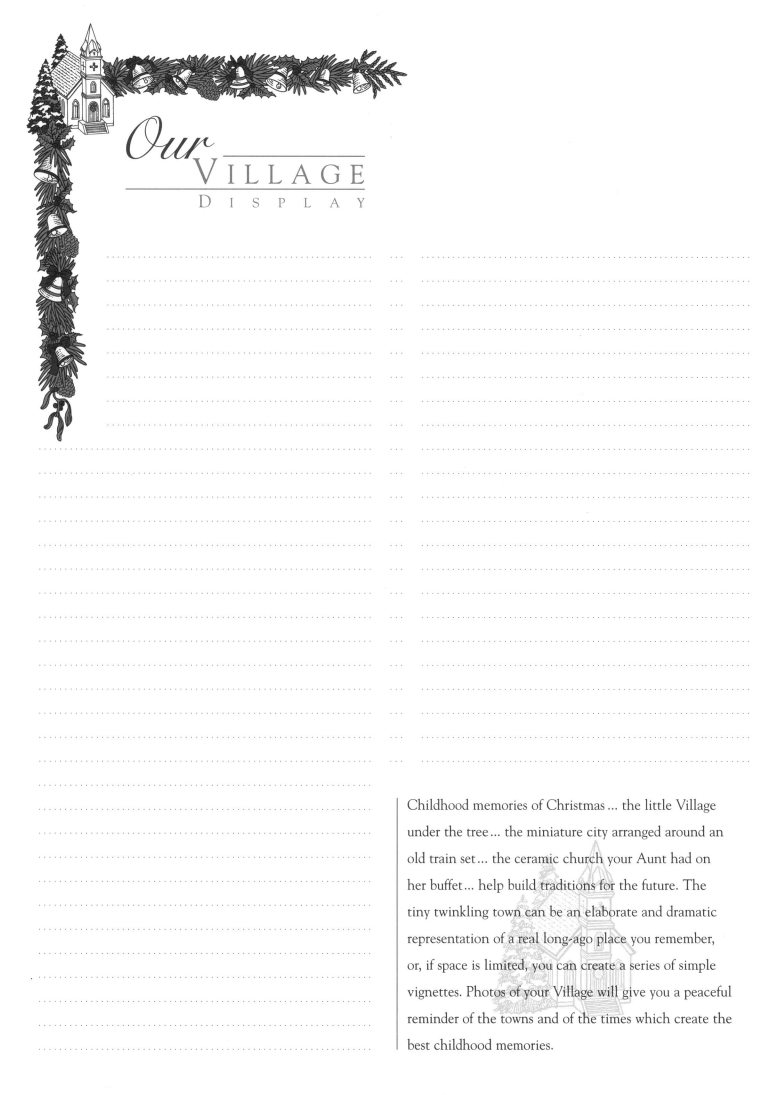

Our
VILLAGE
DISPLAY

Childhood memories of Christmas ... the little Village under the tree ... the miniature city arranged around an old train set ... the ceramic church your Aunt had on her buffet ... help build traditions for the future. The tiny twinkling town can be an elaborate and dramatic representation of a real long-ago place you remember, or, if space is limited, you can create a series of simple vignettes. Photos of your Village will give you a peaceful reminder of the towns and of the times which create the best childhood memories.

This Year's
CHRISTMAS
MEMORIES

Take the time to write down your Christmas remembrances.

Christmas is time for remembering... remembering others

in gifts and acts of kindness... remembering favorite

moments, sure to come when loved ones are gathered

in our homes and in our thoughts. Memories of other

Christmases that contributed to the goodness, the joys,

and the traditions that became part of Christmas today

and will continue the goodness, the joys, and the traditions

of Christmases in years to come.

Things to Remember for
Next Year

Add to the pleasures of next year by taking the few minutes needed to note inspirations and ideas that will ease your planning. Review your preparations for the holiday season just past. This is the time to consider how best to make your next Christmas the most wonderful time ever.

CHRISTMAS

MEMORIES

OF ....

HOLIDAY HOME
DECORATING

Evergreens are inexpensive and a traditional part of holiday decorating. The fragrance and color of fresh boughs are as close as the backyard, garden center, or tree lot. Arrange the greens around a group of tall pillar candles on the coffee table. Add a few pinecones and tuck in some shiny jingle bells. A polished wooden bowl full of apples with sprigs of juniper or boxwood tucked between the fruit looks fresh and inviting on an end table or sideboard. Make your Diary a journal to track changes in your decorations next year.

THE NIGHT BEFORE CHRISTMAS

This is a wonderful night to go caroling. The family or a group of neighbors all ages can bring Christmas joy singing merry songs around the block. Everyone knows the melodies and the words to holiday carols, but print up song cards in case someone forgets. Make arrangements to go to a retirement center—bring fresh baked cookies and other goodies. Your gifts of song and food will be happily remembered throughout the year.

CHRISTMAS DAY

As you enjoy this most traditional holiday, it's nice to think about the reasons you celebrate the way you do. Think about what traditions inspire your decorations, the way you open your gifts, the menu. Discuss it with your family and guests during the day and write a little history in your Diary.

Holiday HOME DECORATING

T H E *Night* B E F O R E C H R I S T M A S

Our
CHRISTMAS
CARD

CHRISTMAS
Day

The
CHRISTMAS
TABLE

The
CHRISTMAS
MENU

....
....
....
....
....
....
....
....
....
....
....
....
....
....
....
....
....
....
....
....
....
....
....

Guests ....
....
....
....
....
....
....
....

Our VILLAGE
DISPLAY

This Year's CHRISTMAS MEMORIES

Things to Remember for Next Year

CHRISTMAS MEMORIES OF ....

HOLIDAY HOME
DECORATING

Decorating our homes for the holidays is a creative, pleasurable process that can be the result of ideas gathered throughout the year. Magazines are ongoing sources of decorating tips, as are store displays, even other homes. Clip articles; jot down ideas you may want to try and save them in your Diary. After the holidays take time to evaluate what worked best and why.

THE NIGHT BEFORE
CHRISTMAS

A lot of tradition involves Christmas Eve. And in
tradition comfort is found. An easy supper is simple to
clear away. Neighbors stop by with gifts or holiday wishes.
Older members of the family read the Christmas story,
A Christmas Carol, or tell how Christmas was celebrated
when grandparents were young. Time to hang the stockings.
Time to turn out the lights. Time to go to bed and dream
of the wonderful day to come.

CHRISTMAS DAY

An old adage claims it is better to give than to receive—
it is also more fun. The approaching holiday season isn't
always the best time to try to think of the perfect gift for
a diverse group of people of all ages with widely differing
tastes. The perfect gift can often present itself in a flash—
anytime of the year. Write it down or better yet, buy it on
the spot. Old interesting bottles purchased at a flea market
can be filled with herb vinegars made from recipes clipped
from magazines.

Holiday HOME Decorating

The *Night* BEFORE CHRISTMAS

Our CHRISTMAS CARD

CHRISTMAS
Day

The CHRISTMAS TABLE

The
CHRISTMAS
MENU

Guests

Our VILLAGE
DISPLAY

This Year's CHRISTMAS MEMORIES

Things to Remember for Next Year

CHRISTMAS MEMORIES OF

....

Preparations don't have to be limited to the weeks just preceding the holiday season. Flowers and herbs gathered from the garden, a field, or the farmers market in summer can be dried and tucked carefully into a Christmas wreath or mantel greens. These will be welcome and colorful memories of summer sunshine. Take photos and keep them in your Christmas Diary as reminders of your beautiful creations.

THE NIGHT BEFORE CHRISTMAS

If there is going to be a lot of guests on Christmas Day, tonight might be your last chance to relax. Fix a cup of hot spicy tea, sit back, let the twinkling lights of the tree and the soft glow of your miniature Village cast a spell. Enjoy a brief and quiet moment. It's almost Christmas.

A feast for the senses and the spirit. Keep the camera handy at all times. Because Christmas Day can bring many friends and family members together, it is the perfect day for a group portrait. A copy of the picture gives everyone, even those who weren't able to attend, a lasting memento of the day. Don't forget the special unposed moments— this is the day filled with occasions for wonderful candid shots. Put a teenager in charge of finding the most memorable photo opportunities and taking the pictures.

Holiday HOME DECORATING

....
....
....
....
....
....
....
....
....
....
....
....
....
....
....
....
....
....
....
....
....
....
....
....
....
....
....
....

The Night Before Christmas

Our CHRISTMAS CARD

CHRISTMAS
Day

The CHRISTMAS TABLE

The
CHRISTMAS
M E N U

Guests

Our VILLAGE
DISPLAY

This Year's
CHRISTMAS
MEMORIES

Things to Remember for Next Year

C H R I S T M A S

MEMORIES

O F

HOLIDAY HOME
DECORATING

Often simple things, already at hand or easily found, take on a new look with a different approach. Check gift stores and tag sales throughout the year to find a group of angels —ornaments, figurines; cloth, china, wood, and silver; any and all sizes, a few or a lot; new and old. Grouped together on a glazed mirror or surrounded by silver glittery ribbon, they will provide a heavenly vignette. Make a note in your Diary of special places where you purchased them and special people (a friend, Grandmother) who gave you one for your grouping.

THE NIGHT BEFORE
CHRISTMAS

When everything that can be done is done, put a favorite carol on the stereo and be creative a new way. Write a Christmas poem or a few brief paragraphs about family—something wonderful a child said—or friends—what a friendship means in this season of good cheer. Your thoughts will become always more meaningful as you and your family read them again in the years to come.

CHRISTMAS DAY

After the presents are all unwrapped and the dinner is over, when everyone sits around feeling stuffed, suggest a walk around the neighborhood to admire the outdoor decorations. Whether it's a brisk brief walk or a leisurely stroll, it can be a healthy pleasant alternative to a nap and the start of a new tradition.

Holiday HOME DECORATING

THE Night BEFORE
CHRISTMAS

Our
CHRISTMAS
CARD

CHRISTMAS
Day

....
....
....
....
....
....
....
....
....
....
....
....
....
....
....
....
....
....
....
....
....
....
....
....
....
....
....
....
....
....
....

The
CHRISTMAS
TABLE

The
CHRISTMAS
M E N U

Guests

Our VILLAGE
DISPLAY

Our VILLAGE
DISPLAY
CONTINUED

This Year's
CHRISTMAS
M E M O R I E S

Things to Remember for Next Year

Our traditions honor our past, make our present more meaningful, and help us look to the future with comfort. Passing our Christmas traditions from generation to generation is our way to make our personal history live. Like all good traditions, we hope this Christmas Diary will become a treasured keepsake passed along and enjoyed for many years to come.

KEEPING A RECORD

Keeping a record in pencil of the Christmas cards you send and receive will help you when updating changes in addresses and names as your family and friends move, grow, and marry. When you look back over the years, these lists become guideposts on your journey through the past.

CHRISTMAS CARD LIST

Name ....   *Name* ....   *Name* ....
....
....
....

Name ....   *Name* ....   *Name* ....
....
....
....

Name ....   *Name* ....   *Name* ....
....
....
....

Name ....   *Name* ....   *Name* ....
....
....
....

Name ....   *Name* ....   *Name* ....
....
....
....

Name ....   *Name* ....   *Name* ....
....
....
....

Name ....   *Name* ....   *Name* ....
....
....
....

CHRISTMAS CARD LIST

Name ....

....

....

....

Name ....

....

....

....

Name ....

....

....

....

Name ....

....

....

....

Name ....

....

....

....

Name ....

....

....

....

Name ....

....

....

....

Name ....

....

....

....

Name ....

....

....

....

Name ....

....

....

....

Name ....

....

....

....

Name ....

....

....

....

Name ....

....

....

....

Name ....

....

....

....

Name ....

....

....

....

Name ....

....

....

....

Name ....

....

....

....

Name ....

....

....

....

Name ....

....

....

....

Name ....

....

....

....

Name ....

....

....

....

VILLAGE GIFTS
GIVEN & RECEIVED

Recording a list of the gifts you gave will help you to plan next year's list. Often a Village piece suggests a companion piece. Jot down what you gave each person and what they would like to go with it.

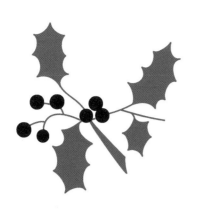

Given To	Year Given	Village	Proper Name	Item #

VILLAGE
GIFTS GIVEN

VILLAGE
GIFTS RECEIVED

Received From	Year Received	Village	Proper Name	Item #